TABLE OF CONTENTS

THE SCRIBAL CROSSROADS 1

WE ARE NOT LIKE EVERYONE ELSE 5

LEARNING THE HARD WAY 9

DEFINING SPEAKING ENGAGEMENTS 15

THE PROPHETIC FOUNDATION OF PRICING
SPEAKING ENGAGEMENTS 21

SETTING YOUR SPEAKER REQUIRMENTS 29

BE REAL ABOUT YOUR ACTUAL EXPENSES 37

COMMON SENSE IS YOUR BEST FRIEND 39

PRICING YOUR SPEAKING ENGAGEMENT 45

SOME HARD-COLD TRUTHS THAT HELPED ME
WITH PRICING 51

SAMPLE SPEAKING TOPICS 59

SETTING PRICING FOR ONLINE SPEAKING 65

How to price your scribal ministry

How to Price Your Scribal Ministry Speaking Engagements

What No One Taught Me I Am Sharing With

THERESA HARVARD JOHNSON

How to Price Your Scribal Ministry Speaking Engagements
Copyright © 2020 Theresa Harvard Johnson
All Rights Reserved. No part of this publication may be reproduced, stored in a retrieval system or transmitted in any form or by any means electronic, mechanical, photocopying, recording or otherwise, without prior written permission of the publisher.

Theresa Harvard Johnson
950 Eagles Landing Parkway, Ste. 302
Stockbridge, GA 30281

"Scripture taken from the New King James Version. Copyright © 1982 by Thomas Nelson, Inc. Used by permission. All rights reserved."

ISBN: 9798684897702
Imprint: Independently published
Printed in the United States of America.

2020 First Edition

If you purchased this book without a cover, you should be aware that this book is stolen property. It is reported as "unsold and destroyed" to the publisher and neither the author, or publisher has received any payment for this stripped book

THE SCRIBAL CROSSROADS

Prophetic Scribes, we stand at a crossroads in our particular niche. Our callings are so broad that what works for popular culture may not work for us - especially those prophetic types who are truly led by the Lord. You see, prophetic people understand that every popular trend, pattern, or matrix for success is not necessarily for them - even if the formula is proven.

Gurus can tell a person how to position themselves to make money by speaking. But is that process in God's plans for you? If it is not, it can become a stumbling block or a path away from God's intention for your life. To be a prophetic scribe is to walk within the design for your life, not the design for everyone else's. The Holy Spirit navigates our path. This is the truth that people who offer advice and insight for masses struggle to understand, that such advice can be a pitfall for prophetic people. Plans that are tailored for us by Holy Spirit often have all kinds of treasures locked in and associated with them that we are destined to uncover.

This is where I step in with counsel and advice for our Scribal Nation™. I wrote this book to help us, especially those prophetic scribes who are just beginning and who long to please God above all else. I have one simple focus in this book: To provide you with the help and tools needed to help price your scribal ministry engagements.

This book is comprised of my personal wisdom, experiences from my own journey and twenty years of insight as a vanguard in the scribal realm, who has equipped thousands of people globally.

My intention is not to give you another formula but to provide practical guidance that fits who we are as a person. Let's face it, we do not have many quality resources that focus exclusively on who and how we are. One of my core mandates is to provide a living repository of quality material to educate, nurture, guide and advance the Scribal Nation.™

Our world has changed.

Ministry, as we have experienced it, will never be the same again, but there will always be opportunities to share our lives in Christ with one another. The key is to be prepared and to stand in expectation of God's best for us within our own "unique" design. Always embrace immersion in Christ!

Embracing Immersion,

Theresa Harvard Johnson, MDIV, MAPW
Founder, The School of the Scribe

How to price your scribal ministry

WE ARE NOT LIKE EVERYONE ELSE

We are not like everyone else!

Take a few minutes to let that statement about us sink in. While some might laugh at it, there will be other believers like me. This declaration is not about having any special or elite position. Rather, it simply infers that we have initiatives and concerns that are unique to us that need to be addressed. We are prophetic scribes - a nation filled with Sons operating at varying levels of scribal gifts with an understanding based on "The Scribal Anointing®" that has never graced the congregation in the measure we see it today. And while the apostolic-prophetic community is awakening to the "truth of who we are," many have yet to grasp it.

This is not negative news.

Rather, it is a way of saying that we are pioneers opening up a new frontier by the leading of the Holy Spirit. We are not simply people who write creatively, administratively, or instructionally, we are people who administrate the Kingdom through varying scribal gifts. Listen, the scribes of the scripture were a class of people with broad areas of specialty.

Saying we are scribes is like saying we are musicians. There are so many different kinds of musicians! To the musician the question becomes, "What kind of musician are you?" same question for the scribe, "What kind of scribe are you?" In our circumstance, we can change that to "prophetic" scribe. Some types of scribes are writers, recorders, editors, publishers, bookkeepers, lawyers, instructors, and the list goes on.

Even more intriguing is this truth: Just as each instrument has a class to which it belongs - like woodwind, string, percussion, so does the scribe. The Scribal Anointing® classes us in three distinctive categories: administrative, instructional, and creative. As we move through this book, keep this truth close to heart because under the "prophetic anointing," there are a wide range of topics for us to dig out that are opening up.

In the coming years, all kinds of specialty areas will emerge where speakers and teachers are needed on varying scales throughout our global communities. You could be among those called to further excavate the scribal realm and pioneer a fresh well in the scribal realm. We really are not like everyone else in our specific type of release!

As I share my heart with you concerning this subject, keep this idea of us being "unique" close. You see, it is your uniqueness and the establishment of it that will set your assignment to speak into others apart. It is your uniqueness that will ultimately create a niche for your message and help you price your speaking engagements.

And if you are already soaring in your scribal realm, the nuggets shared here may help you gain clarity concerning how to not only price your speaking engagements, but model them for expanding opportunities. What I appreciate about this book however, is that it is not a step-by-step or how-to in the traditional sense of telling someone how to do things. Rather, it is filled with insights intended to guide as you seek the Holy Spirit concerning your own process and pattern. We need more of that and maybe less steps in this "age of experts." Let us always be vigilant and ready in our instructed place.

How to price your scribal ministry

LEARNING THE HARD WAY

I was newly saved when people began inviting me to share poetry and spoken word. If you are a creative scribe, chances are that some of your ministry engagements will be rooted in poetry, plays, skits, monologues, and other creative activities like mine were. Those gifts can open wide and effective doors of opportunity.

Back in 2000 and 2001, it was *not common* to have people floating from ministry event to ministry event sharing those types of gifts. I do not mean they did not do it, rather, it was not as popular and accepted as it is today. There were preachers who taught against most forms of the arts that we practice today in the church. Those churches that did embrace the arts, relegated them to in-house service reserved for Easter, Christmas, Mother's Day, Father's Day, Youth Sunday, church anniversary, conventions, women's meetings, and other related programs.

I attended hundreds of conferences during the first decade of my ministry. All of these leaders were pioneering. I was blessed to be among the first in those environments to teach on prophetic writing, and the first to introduce the mantle of the scribe some-time later. My focus was mostly on Levitical worship, liturgical dance, visual art, song, worship, and visual expression.

If traveling was involved, it had two distinct sides: Leaders of church arts groups would go to conferences to learn, participate or be equipped; and creatives in ministry groups traveled within that congregation or their denominational circle. People did not travel at the magnitude they do now, and even fewer received honorariums for it. Back then, everything you did for the Lord was viewed as sacrificial and your reasonable service to Him. Even pastors, especially in the black community of my youth, were at the mercy of offerings, meals, or gifts of those they blessed.

I was equipped under old-school leaders and ministers who viewed ministry from this perspective. If you were a creative, then your creative gifts were a part of the church auxiliary. If you were administrative, then your administrative gifts were assigned to the administration of the church or auxiliary events. If you were instructional, then your teaching gifts were used in

Sunday school, Bible studies, church auxiliaries, special services, church support groups, healing circles, prayer teams or positioned to be trained as a preacher or minister.

What you did not see were a ton of ministries independent of the local church! And up until 2015, the term "prophetic scribe" was still a whisper across the prophetic community moving from the invisible to the visible. Even now, we continue to await its massive surge globally with the depth of understanding that "The Scribal Anointing®" provides.

When we consider the local church, specifically in the United States, we learn that all ministry have been traditionally centered on a strong pastoral hierarchy - even in the speaking engagement arena. Outside of that structure, it *has only been within the 21st century* that we have seen such a push toward "Christian speakers" as we do now.

What I have shared is not judgment on the generation before us, but a declaration concerning how things have changed. This century ushered in a new era of ministry - one that has made room for speakers who specialize in a plethora of different, non-traditional areas of ministry foreign to the previous generation in their release at this level, and this includes the prophetic scribe. The Scribal Conservatory Arts & Worship Center and The School of the Scribe stand as profound examples of this! It's fully a fresh example of the direction the congregation is moving toward, which is also an expressive organization, focused on education in the scribal arts.

My first speaking engagement outside of the local church paradigm was in 2001. I was a baby Christian - about eight months saved and was asked to do "prophetic" spoken word poems on healing from sexual abuse. I was paid in hugs, appreciation, standing ovations, encouragement and more effective doors of opportunity that took me across my city, state, country and eventually internationally. "I didn't know anything about traveling and speaking when I started! I learned the hard way - through trial and error," but you don't have to.

The pastors and leaders around me loved the scribal gift but did not understand it or me. To them, I was not a real "minister" with real "ministry concerns." While many who knew me then, can see the reward today... I was alone in my process. There were no mentors in the "scribal arts - outside of publishing" for me that could grasp the vision of the Scribal Nation™.

Back then, everything a person did for the Lord was viewed as sacrificial. When the time finally came to accept larger and broader ministry engagements, I had to trust God through my development. I ended up serving in two global traveling ministries in which I gleaned from their event planning efforts. I saw how they managed guest ministers, developed contracts and agreements for their own requests, and the Lord began to teach me the good, the bad and the ugly. I learned to position and present myself for godly opportunities, I learned to ask the right questions when invited, how to develop and send speaking agreements, and how to teach people to honor not just the gift in me but the calling on my life.

I took what I learned to heart, transformed it for my purposes and introduced it into our scribal culture - helping scribes not only make sense of their worth, but package themselves in a way that set standards of treatment in their lives. Sometimes, you have to TEACH PEOPLE how to honor you whether your ministry is voluntary or missional, where everything is free, within a ministry network or by speaker invitation where honorariums and fees may apply.

There is no judgment here concerning how you walk out your calling. FREE IS GREAT if that is your volunteer or missional journey. There is also nothing wrong with ministers having fees associated with their services. I have multiple curriculums, and an educational center. By design, what I do requires tuition fees within ancient and modern educational models among biblical scribes.

Many people are not aware that it was common for certain classes of scribes to receive payment for teaching and educating their pupils in the pre and post Christ. They are not aware that some scribes receive housing, the king's protection, and payment for their services.

Here are some take-a-ways from this chapter that can help you navigate:

- You are not alone in navigating your scribal journey
- Speaking engagements are not just for certain leaders, they include creatives
- Your assignment and calling is valuable to the Lord
- The 21st century is revolutionizing the congregation
- The role of the prophetic scribe is critical in this dispensation of the church
- Some prophetic scribes are emerging pioneers
- Learn from the mistakes and successes of those who have gone before you
- Teach people how to honor the assignment upon your life
- Freely embrace your assignment and respect the choice of others to embrace theirs
- Certain classes of scribes were paid to teach and train others in the scribal arts
- Walk out the destiny the Lord has assigned to you

DEFINING SPEAKING ENGAGEMENTS

Globally, speaking engagements are defined as speaking before groups of people on a specific subject you are knowledgeable about, for the purpose of informing, motivating or otherwise encouraging them whether paid or free. Speaking engagements are equated with giving sermons, lectures, or speeches across various platforms either in person or virtual.

If you are a scribe - especially a pioneering one in your family or community, I want to challenge you to see what you do publicly as a prophetic poet and spoken word artist *as public speaking*. It is not just formal speeches and sermons. If we are going to have a legitimate expectation of being received from a place of financial value, then we must change how we see ourselves as "creative scribes."

Creatives have spent too much time on the "outskirts" of speaking engagements, focusing on performances and gigs. A performance and gig mindset, in the scribal realm, often locks people into a certain type of mindset for opportunities. It will also lock you into certain financial brackets related to speaking – especially when starting out.

Prophetic scribes are different – on multiple levels! We have the creative, administrative, and instructional realms that we can navigate in the public relations arena. In addition, we are ministers of the Lord first and foremost, not second. Do we use and manipulate the "prophetic" only to receive material for a show, performance, or conference event? Some people do, and they are correct in saying they are performing or going to their next gig.

However, those involved in *pure ministry* are building around a ministry mission or vision that ties to a goal in seeing the Lord's intention fulfilled not only in their lives, but in the lives of others. How WE THINK ABOUT THIS matters!

These are the avenues for speaking engagements that I have walked through as a prophetic scribe over the years. I have been:

- Invited to minister with a team of poets I formed through poetry and spoken word

- Invited to minister poetry and spoken word for special ministry/secular related events
- Invited to teach on The Scribal Anointing®, the office of the prophetic scribe (for two to three-day sessions as the only speaker), often followed by preaching a Sunday morning message (non-related to scribes)
- Invited to teach in private sessions with two-five leaders on building prophetic scribal teams
- Invited to teach on the scribal arts (workshops, special sessions, keynotes)
- Invited to speak on topics related to healing from sexual abuse, mental illness (in secular and sacred settings where I've always opened with poetry from my own journey of healing)
- Invited to speak at women's conferences (varying issues & topics, have included relevant prophetic poetry)
- Invited to host one or two-day workshops on specific scribal topics (dreams/visions, memoir writing, etc.)
- Invited to host one-day scribe schools in "schools of the prophets"
- Invited to speak on building/guiding prophetic scribal teams in a church setting
- Invited to speak on building/guiding prophetic scribal teams as mainstream ministry
- Invited to speak on apostolic/prophetic panels concerning the direction of the worship, arts & the church

- Invited to speak about my journalism career and experience at public schools
- Invited to teach writing/art workshops at retreats for sex-trafficking survivors (children/adults)
- Invited specifically to share poetry with children and/or teens about abuse
- Invited to speak about the subjects in the books I have authored, and so on
- Invited to share a poem at weddings, funerals, and memorials
- Invited to speak at family reunion events
- Invited to emcee arts related events
- Invited to play a key role in plays, skits, monologues, etc.
- Invited to write and record original, narrative poetry for scenes in plays and skits

While reading this, I hope you are taking an inventory of the speaking engagements you have had. Perhaps, you are considering the type of speaking engagements you see in your future and/or are being awakened to opportunities you have not considered. In looking at this list, I hope you can see that how viewing what you are called to do as a prophetic scribe, might be considered differently from a "performance" or a "gig."

As a prophetic scribe, I would pick up a burden for the people for many of the things I was invited to participate in. For years, this was my confirmation to accept the opportunity. When there was no burden, I simply made the choice to go if there was no check or warning to decline resonating from my Spirit. We must understand that being "prophetic" scribes is not just about hearing God but understanding what He wants to impart from the message of your life in those "sacred times" into the lives of others.

It is here that we begin to consider how to price our scribal ministry engagements. Note, however, that the insight I am providing is primarily from the perspective of ministry - although there is wisdom that can be applied for many types of opportunities.

How to price your scribal ministry

THE PROPHETIC FOUNDATION OF PRICING SPEAKING ENGAGEMENTS

Relationships are everything!

If there is one piece of advice I can give up front, this is the one I pray those reading hold on to more than the others: Seek to cultivate relationships over simply seeking to secure a speaking engagement.

Ecclesiastes 4:7-10 NIV says, "Again I saw something meaningless under the sun: There was a man all alone; he had neither son nor brother. There was no end to his toil, yet his eyes were not content with his wealth. "For whom am I toiling," he asked, "and why am I depriving myself of enjoyment?" This too is meaningless - a miserable business! Two are better than one, because they have a good return for their labor: If either of them falls down, one can help the other up. But woe to anyone who falls and has no one to help them up."

The most fundamental principles I have adopted about doing anything in the Kingdom, revolve around relationship building.

If this is what is most important in the foundation of our faith (Matthew 22:34-40) then it must also be our foundation. The Kingdom moves on loving, helping, and bearing the burdens of ministry with one another, not on the hireling mindset (John 10:12-16).

There are three types of relationships that *helped me* decide HOW TO PRICE MY SPEAKING ENGAGEMENTS. I know this might sound strange but hear me out, it makes sense for those whose hearts are pure, and ministry led.

They are:

- CLOSE MUTUALLY-EDIFYING RELATIONSHIPS. These are relationships that earnestly reflect God's intentions for you and are intimate, stable contributors and nurturers of your success like your family, pastor, mentor, and trustworthy friends who believe in what you bring to the table. If you are blessed to have these relationships, then they can be a tremendous source of opportunity -

especially when you are starting out. In mutually edifying relationships, we can freely share our gifts without any expectation of financial compensation. If the mutually edifying friend desires to be a blessing to your life, allow them to do so. These are the relationships focused on "sharing life together" - including ministry.

For example, if my mentor is hosting a conference, I readily volunteer - whether the need is serving as a workshop or keynote presenter or setting up the vending area. Many times, these mutually edifying relationships have led to my expertise being recommended to others as I have them. You can make tremendous strides in gaining speaking experience, perfecting your expert knowledge base, building credibility, meeting new people, bartering services, training your speaking etiquette and developing your brand through these relationships.

While there may be minimal to no financial compensation, what you gain is a small circle of people who really know your work ethic and expertise; and who can testify willingly and joyfully to your skill and ability. You have the opportunity to "grow with others" here into their brotherly and prosperous place, so do not despise the days of small beginnings.

This was AND continues to be a huge place of service for me. You see, I mentor established leaders as well as those just starting out. Because I have a niche, a base and following at this stage of my life, I practice this with them. They have open invitations to speak at my conferences and events, mingle with the people I lead and get whatever experience they need while I support and encourage them. In addition, if they have a conference and need a keynote speaker or workshop presenter, not only do I volunteer but I have cultivated a team of people who will fall right in and help them, easing the financial burden while presenting non-competitive help and support at no cost to them.

- MINISTRY CONNECTIONS WITH LIKE-MINDED LEADERS. Consider finding somewhere to serve and volunteer within your community or abroad. Missional work and focus can be a profound launching ground for emerging speakers. I have volunteered with all kinds of non-profit organizations over the years. By volunteering, I was able to combine three passions at once: (1) serving broken and hurting children and adults in my community; (2) cultivating the scribal and artistic gifts through spirit-led activities for children, youth and adults, and (3) teaching people about the goodness of God regardless of their circumstances and situations.

Over time other, paid opportunities emerged from my volunteer activity that moved me deeper into my purpose. I volunteered at domestic violence shelters, sexual exploitation recovery programs and foster-care related youth service organizations. You do not have to have a lot of time! The time you give, however, needs to be meaningful, professional and most of all consistent. I served once a month at the domestic violence shelter for over a year - working with women who survived domestic violence. I served with the sexual exploitation recovery programs for over seven years working with children, teens, and adults for a seven-day onsite retreat, twice a year.

I spent the rest of the year gathering donations, organizing scribes to make journals for each guest, and raising funds to supply the participants with quality gifts. I used my poetry open mics, conferences for prophetic writers, etc. to promote the cause of these organizations, sell their products, solicit volunteers, and even opened up meetings for advocates to talk about the cause. This opened the door for me to speak at university campuses, before law enforcement and medical professionals for a season on helping survivors recover and heal. CREATE THE DOOR TO THE OPPORTUNITIES YOU SEEK WITHIN YOUR SCRIBAL MINISTRY! THE HOLY SPIRIT HAS GIVEN YOU THE WISDOM TO DO SO!

- **PARTNER WITH MINISTRIES, ORGANIZATIONS & BUSINESSES THAT NEED WHAT YOU HAVE.** Build relationships with those whose client base you serve. To do this, however, may sometimes require deliberate effort on your part to network.

This means presenting yourself to these business professionals via social media platforms, professional organizations or societies, meetups, joining speaker bureaus relevant to your field, or scheduling virtual or in-person meetings to present what you offer.

While God can and does create opportunities for people without all the bells and whistles, it doesn't hurt to package who you are and what you do to clearly define who you are and what you offer as a prophetic scribe. To begin this process, I strongly suggest developing a simple, professional web presence, obtaining branded business cards, setting up social media accounts that you keep active concerning your business, setting up a marketplace or store to sell products, and making sure your most important client testimonials and experience (if possible) are well documented on those pages. Sometimes, it is in this space that we can begin developing a rate sheet or pricing plan as a reference for what we offer.

Most importantly, please CHOOSE what works within your "prophetic scribal dimension." Remember, just because it worked for Susan and Joe does not mean it is going to work for you no matter how great it is! Prophetic people have a path (not just for wealth), but for knowledge, equipping and exploration that they must take. We can miss divine training and opportunities by doing things "our way" or by the way of "the guru." The blessing of "systems" do not look or present themselves the same as the blessings of the "prophetic." You can take that to the bank. I have experienced CRAZY FAVOR – things money cannot buy at the hands of people, businesses, and organizations.

With the right motives, prayer, and wise counsel, you can set the foundation for a prosperous speaking ministry around your scribal calling. It is critical to understand, however, how important relationships can be to your success if you learn to cultivate them from a place of mutuality.

Sometimes, you might put more into those relationships that you are getting out of them. But if you are patient, meeting people where they are with mutual respect, time will release some profound rewards. Your prophetic movements can be far more valuable than a GURU's plan, especially when navigating an area of ministry that so people may NEED TO SEE or experience what is inside you to understand.

The three points shared can be viewed as ways to prayerfully position certain relationships in your life. Most people cultivate at least two of these types of relationships simultaneously anyway if their ear is tuned to the Spirit. I operate in cultivating mutually edifying relationships and mutually beneficial partnerships with ministries, businesses, and organizations continuously. Why? Because we meet new people every day who bring new experiences, knowledge and opportunities that can challenge us to stretch and grow.

ONE THING IS SURE: Relationship building WILL BE a central catalyst of your success as a public or private speaker. It is how the Kingdom and the world works.

On a final note, one of the greatest lies prophetic scribes must overcome is thinking that EXPERIENCE determines how much you are worth as it relates to speaking engagements.

THIS IS WRONG!

This may have been true 20-years ago but not applicable today. What matters is that you know your craft, understand how to connect to your audience and can do so efficiently, effectively and with the integrity of Christ. NEVER forget this! We are no longer bound by those rules. You CAN EARN an expert's "fee" if you can fulfill the requirements of the speaking engagement. Never allow ANYONE to tell you otherwise.

SETTING YOUR SPEAKER REQUIRMENTS

When in pure ministry (ministry without ungodly motives), there are reasonable requirements that should be met when you are invited to speak. Defining these requirements, specifically those that are necessary concerning your travel and service, vary depending on individual and organization.

Speaking requirements refer to "what you have need for" if an individual, group or organization plans to have you speak at their event. From a Sonship perspective, this is not about greed or extravagance. Rather, it is about worth, honor and respect. Period. I beg you! Do not become one of those people who abuse the privilege to serve others. I did not write this book for those kinds of people!

1 Timothy 5:17-18 says, "The elders who direct the affairs of the church well are worthy of double honor, especially those whose work is preaching and teaching. For Scripture says, "Do not muzzle an ox while it is treading out the grain, and the worker deserves his wages."

It is important to know that there is:

- **Information every speaker should collect immediately after receiving a speaking engagement.** This information includes the organization's name, address, phone number, email address, social media information, as well as the full name of the primary contact(s). Depending on your relationship with the contact, it is ideal to use this information not only to pray but to research the individual, business, or organization. A simple Google and social media search is generally sufficient. These extra steps could also protect your good name and any credibility you may have established. One of the greatest benefits of building relationships is that people you trust can refer you or you can meet new people by relationship. Research may also confirm whether or not what you offer is a good fit for the potential engagement and whether or not you are a good fit for them.

- **Detailed information about the event that you may need beyond the basics.** I want to take a few minutes to talk about this because, at least for me, it is critical. You need to know: Who is hosting the event or is it a collaborative effort among different groups? You want to be sure that the event is representative of who you are and who you are becoming. So, make sure you are CLEAR about what-is-what? Ambiguity should not cloud your speaking engagement; rest assured that well-known speakers vet their engagements well.

If there are multiple speakers and presenters, especially keynote, ask who they are. If they are well-known, it plays a huge role in the budget and/or connections associated with this opportunity. Ask about past conferences, events, search the social media sites. Some people may believe this is "too much" but it is not. Years ago, I attended a ministry event as a poet and workshop presenter.

I taught for three-hours and released poetry before an audience of 2,000 people who paid registration fees to be there at an evening service. I was given $250 for that effort. That would have been great for a group of 50 or less. Hear me out... as this is real talk.

There were three keynote speakers, one of whom was well known, a famous worship team and performing artists, etc. The keynote speaker received about $10k for the evening service. The others received $2,500 and all received expenses, hotel, meals, and travel. I paid my own way to this event but was not offered so much as a bottle of water, or access to the

Green Room.

In retrospect, I realize I set myself up for this treatment. I did not know the conference protocols, what questions to ask, or how to present myself at this event. Should the conference planners have asked? Well, they did. They asked me to send my requirements. I asked for an honorarium of *their choosing*. I did not know what that question meant or how to appropriately respond, and they did not explain. That was a hard lesson to learn!

In "non-ministry settings," the protocols are different. Generally, contracts are given by the conference or event host that will outline what they expect and what they will provide the guest speaker with - which includes any agreed upon necessities provided by the speaker. Veterans in the speaking industry have contracts they provide to the conference host or event planner or they use "speaker bureaus or booking agencies" to avoid the complexity of dealing with this issue. Some people have dedicated and seasoned assistants who take care of these details and handle the negotiations. It is my prayer that you learn from some of my mistakes. Sometimes people muzzle us (and I have some dramatic stories), and sometimes we muzzle ourselves out of ignorance, fear and/or lack of understanding of our own worth.

- **Ask how many people will be in attendance and note if there is a registration fee.** At the same event mentioned above, attendees paid registration fees ranging from $89 - $249. Many times, especially in ministry, potential speakers ask this question. This is not a "nosey" question, but a question that helps them determine two things: 1. If 2,000 people are present and the average person pays $89, the conference could generate an excess of $180k. This doesn't include any special sessions or product sales - and if it's a ministry event, there will be at least one offering. If every person gave a $50 offering that evening, that would be an additional $100k.

I have been a part of "planning meetings" that generated millions and people walked away with speaker fees in excess of $25-$50k for half-day workshops. These are people, however, who have the name, influence and semi-celebrity status to garner speaking fees of this caliber. Take Oprah Winfrey for example. Her average speaking fee is just under $400k per engagement whereas Cornel West and Connie Chung average $50k per engagement (Source: Booking Entertainment).

Most speakers will never move into this speaking engagement income bracket. This is not a lack of faith or the words of a pessimist, but a true statement. In addition, they will probably

How to price your scribal ministry

speak at a private event, Ivy league schools, elite organizations, etc. for the most part with people whose individual and organizational wealth bracket fits their speaker fees. By sharing this information with you, I hope to broaden the view of the "speaking potential" that is before us.

- **Ask if there will be vending opportunities and adequate time to do so**. If you have products, it is always good to present them if they are appropriate for the event. This is especially true in situations where the conference or the event host does not meet the preferred honorarium. Many, MANY TIMES I have sold products to off-set my travel expenses with conferences and events. You can as well if you have quality products. Organizations should be able to provide as much information as possible for the engagement and communicate significant changes. This is professional, courteous, and honoring to the speaker.

In addition, there should be an honorific exchange that should take place between the individual, ministry, or organization.

- **Finally, I also ask this question: Will there be opportunities to connect with the conference host and speakers?** In ministry, there is usually time for this because "real ministry is relational." It is not, however, always common or possible in secular arenas. We commonly see people finish their speaking engagement, spend some time greeting the guests, etc., but they promptly leave afterwards.

Remember, the information gathered is critical to helping you determine how to price your speaking engagements. One final note on this topic: Speakers generally collect this information by placing it in a form or sending an email to the conference or event host. Check out my simple online "speaker request form" to see how I address these questions and more: https://rb.gy/cwqgy0. Just type this link into your web browser.

How to price your scribal ministry

BE REAL ABOUT YOUR ACTUAL EXPENSES

Listen, this is real talk.

I am married. My husband is an essential worker managing a 9AM-5PM shift to help support our family. I am a full-time pastor over a set group of people. I am also an entrepreneur with multiple streams of income. Before the pandemic, I traveled up to 8-10 days a month, sometimes more. There are expenses I incur at home that must be offset.

For example, I have a son with severe special needs. One of two things must take place when I travel: My husband has to take time from work to care for him, or I have to arrange a sitter for every day I am away. In addition, my husband sometimes goes to work late because he has to drive me to the airport when I am traveling out of state or I take a taxi or other service. He loses more time at work and/or I pay $75 one way to taxi to the airport.

Realistically, it could cost my family $500 just for me to leave home (loss of salary and specialized childcare) If I was working a full-time position, I would lose that time at work as well. What scenario are you facing? Even if auntie or grandma could watch the children for free, it does not matter. This is STILL a realistic and necessary consideration.

COMMON SENSE IS YOUR BEST FRIEND

One of the most frustrating aspects of deciding what to charge is not simply "looking at the going rate" for speaking engagements. This is good, but it is not everything. You also need to consider how "the prices you set" will impact your current circumstances - especially when traveling for ministry. If ever there was a place to "be scammed, mistreated and abused" as it relates to conferences, events and speaking engagements, ministry is that place!

I am being honest here.

Maybe one day I will share some of my horrible experiences and lessons learned with rising pastors and leaders to help prepare them for the journey. It is important for you to teach people how to "treat" you. Because my ministry model is relational, I often stay in the comfortable, private homes of ministers I know well when I travel - especially internationally.

The key, however, is that the hosts understand the need for privacy, peace, quiet and rest as it relates to your speaking engagement; and will not turn the time in their home into a circus (frenzied children, bringing friends over for private ministry, prophecy meeting for family, unannounced dinner parties, etc.). Because of this, I generally recommend hotel stays to avoid such confusion and unintended offense. If there are great boundaries and the relationships are mutually edifying, this can be great.

With that said, speakers need to decide whether or not their travel expenses are included in their speaking fees or separated from them. This is very important and needs to be made clear. For example, if a speaker sets $2,500 as the fee for a one-day conference (4-6-hour training), is this the check for their service? Or is it an all-inclusive price from which hotel, transportation, meals, etc. will be calculated? People have some unique ideas about how they approach speaker fees. Make sure you are clear on it, before finalizing your plans.

In general, the following travel expenses should be separate from your speaking fees:

- FLIGHTS

- Be sure to recommend your preferred airline and provide your rewards number. If traveling abroad, this might not always be possible. Be flexible with seating. Humility does not make demands or release undue burdens upon people.

- HOTEL RESERVATIONS
    - Be sure to recommend your preferred hotel and provide your rewards number. Your safety and health are important. Choose accommodations whenever possible that provide both. Be prepared, however, to arrive in areas that do not have those options or choices, especially if traveling internationally. I have TONS of small-town stories! Do your research.

- BAGGAGE & EQUIPMENT FEES
    - Be sure to "insist" that luggage/baggage fees are covered. Cheap flights often exclude these and can leave travelers paying an additional $100 one-way. If you travel with "special equipment" that is critical to your assignment, include this as well.

- MEALS
    - Be sure to have meals covered. This is especially important for dietary concerns when health is an issue. It is not always feasible for organizations to

accommodate restrictive diets. So, having the option to purchase "what you can eat" should be considered.

- GROUND TRANSPORTATION
  - Be sure to include any transportation fees including mileage, taxi and or car rental fees.

Three realistic options apply here: 1. The speaker covers the expenses, and the hosting individual, ministry or organization reimburses the speaker. *(Avoid this option if possible.);* (2) The hosting individual, ministry or organization covers the expenses in advance; or (3) The hosting individual, ministry, or organization states in advance what they will and will not cover. This is very, very common. When this happens, it is necessary to have the level of grace and humility to negotiate or accept the terms presented. Not every opportunity operates like they do in the "apostolic-prophetic" community. We are a special group of people as it relates to how some groups approach this subject.

In secular arenas, these things are spelled out in contractual agreements. BUT AT A MINIMUM, speakers should always consider each engagement on a per assignment basis. You do not want to incur a $1k in expenses and receive a $600 honorarium. Obviously, some things would not apply to local speaking engagements.

WHAT DO YOU BRING TO THE TABLE?

Here is another important point in this discussion. Perhaps the greatest hurdle associated with pricing speaking engagements is having *an accurate view* of what YOU bring to the table. While experience and credentials can be important, they are not always signs of a person's worth or capabilities. I mentioned this before, but it needs to be said again: *Experience alone does not guarantee or even warrant success in this arena! Not in the times in which we live.*

This means that some people can get started exactly where they are and grow into the experience, earn the credentials, and acquire the skill as they go. I am STILL learning, earning, and growing - after twenty years! However, I have learned that speaking engagements are geared toward how much those inviting you value what you bring to the table.

A seven-minute poem from the late Maya Angelou may be worth $15-20k dollars. Whereas a poem from a local poet in your community might garner transportation costs only, a gift certificate for a nice dinner or an honorarium of $75 - $200.

Use the "Brainstorming Speaking Topics" worksheet at the end of this book for ideas on how to determine what you bring to the table and how to set your exact fees.

PRICING YOUR SPEAKING ENGAGEMENT

I mentioned this previously: Experience, especially in the secular realm, does not always guarantee or even warrant success in the speaking arena. In this age of social media, people are unknown one-day and an overnight sensation the next.

It happens and will continue to happen as long as social media inserts itself as a staple of society globally.

However, ministry is somewhat different - especially within the apostolic-prophetic community. I have been traveling since 2001. I began on the poet/spoken word artist circuit around Atlanta and at local churches across the southern United States. If you do not know what that means, it simply indicates that I was heavily involved in evangelistic style ministry at local cafes, clubs and other venues where they staged popular open mic poetry nights. Poets literally walked into the venues, signed their name on a list to perform, and released their poetry before a crowd of strangers. This was a passion for me. Back then, Atlanta was a hotspot for poets, spoken word artists and slam poetry.

Without a doubt ministry experience, credentials, reputation, influence, area of expertise and even one's honor within the community play a role in the honorarium; or what you present as a request or point of negotiation. You can take this to the bank! Reverence, honor, influence (if you have it) within your measure is the "secret-sauce" often associated with one's success with speaking engagements. A person whose service is in demand is generally rising or is established in the area they bring to the table in ministry settings.

It is so important for those who are positioning themselves as speakers to:

- Refine the message. For example, as a prophetic scribe I am known globally within my sphere of influence for my teachings on The Scribal Anointing®, the revelation of "the office" of the prophetic scribe. Know what areas you specialize in. As a poet, most of my writing dealt with healing from deep brokenness from sexual assault and abuse. Everything began for me in that place and expanded as I developed and grew in the Lord.

- Prove the message. For example, The Scribal Anointing® focuses on digging out the identity of the prophetic scribe, defining scribal purpose and providing a roadmap concerning how to navigate the office. With the Holy Spirit, an entire repository has been developed around these three areas that is constantly expanding. Whether you have arrived in this place or not, it is critical to build resources around your message that are useful and unique – whether as books, bookmarks, or a podcast.

- Become the expert. For example, position yourself where you will get to know your subject matter well. If you have a gift that is common, look for that "edge" that separates you from everyone else. The Holy Spirit is an expert at that when we devote our time to considering our portion. For example, my teachings on the scribe are "tailored to scribal foundations" - areas that are mostly unknown and fragmented at this time by most people journeying in scribal ministry. In my niche, which I had to create from scratch, it is in demand in this day and time. It is therefore important for me to keep developing needed resources and nurturing the community.

- Create a consistent and strong presence on social media

and the Internet. As you bloom, make sure you have all necessary collateral to support your vision. Be able to be found! This is what I mean by that statement. Start with a blog, a book and business cards if you are just beginning. Be as professional as possible in your presentation and conversation. But above all be *consistent and faithful* through the good, bad, and ugly seasons of your journey. Longevity, consistency, and adaptation to change are KEYS to building your influence and presenting your value! Do not wait for people to invite YOU! Begin hosting your own events, conferences, etc. virtually and in person.

- Create the community you do not have! If no one knows your name, build the tribe you would like to see. I started with a Yahoo Group for poets nearly 20 years ago. Many of those who joined way back then are still following me today. If people do know you, begin organizing them around your message. Let them know HOW you can help them or provide a solution for some areas of their lives. I provide tools to help prophetic scribes understand who they are in the Lord and embrace that identity. It is that simple.

There's so much more I could say, but I believe this is great info concerning increasing your "marketablility." Please understand that your WORTH is rooted in Christ and is non-debatable. There is, however, a monetary value on the mind, wisdom, skill and gifts that are presented at the table of people.

Again, an eight-minute poem from the late Maya Angelou might have garnered $15-$50K depending on the audience. Whereas a poem from an unknown local poet in the community with a current, limited audience and without any literary prizes or awards might garner transportation costs and a $50 - $100 honorarium. On average, however, a workshop presenter at beginner level, could expect to set a rate of $50-$150 an hour.

An experienced workshop presenter might set a rate of $250-$350 per hour or $750-$1K for a half day. At a minimum, a seasoned presenter might set a rate of $1,500 - $2,500 a day and up for a full day workshop depending on the meeting size, venue, and budget. This is in addition to other expenses which are separate as we have already discussed. For more days and larger groups, it's always better to negotiate.

Sometimes, ministry related conferences that host multiple workshops may not offer speaker compensation. If they do, it might not even be significant. The reward is often paid in exposure, teaching experience, having the opportunity to sell products without vending fees, being listed in promotions and networking.

Keynote speaker honorariums in ministry environments can range from $500 to $2,500 *at the minimum*. Larger venues and audiences can easily increase the worth of that engagement. Check out the worksheet, "SPEAKING ENGAGEMENT CATEGORIES & EXPENSES" worksheet at the end of this book.

SOME HARD-COLD TRUTHS THAT HELPED ME WITH PRICING

We are engaging in real talk!

My intention is not to discourage anyone from their speaking endeavors. However, I need to say this again: *We must have a right perception of ourselves and what we offer (Romans 12:3).*

- **Highly sought-after speakers are chosen for their area of expertise, not randomness.** If you do not have a "specialty area" you are probably not ready to take the speaking arena by storm. People are selected for "what they know" and can "impart." Ask yourself this question: What is my area of expertise? Your area of expertise needs to be made clear. Check out my "Brainstorming Speaking Topics" handout at the end of this book. It goes over the topics I can speak on easily and with evidence in my life. I have books, videos from conferences, audio files, etc. that can prove every topic on this list along with endorsements from leaders who invited me. Do not be intimidated by this list; I have been speaking publicly and consistently for two-decades.

- **One speaking fee or speakers fee outline is NOT enough.** There is no one-size-fits-all. We are PROPHETIC - there is a difference in how we approach and walk out this area. Read, study, and learn how speaking engagements work. Serious and experienced speakers will develop a fee scale - not a one-price-fits-all model. First, there are numerous kinds of speaking engagements - workshops, seminars, conferences, ministry engagements, etc. Secondly, there are always issues of times and days. One group might require two-hours of your time, while others might require multiple overnight stays. Most of my speaking engagements span two-three days. It is helpful to consider hourly rates as well.

- **Do not ignore your travel expenses!** I talked about this previously. I highly recommend keeping this completely separate from any discussion concerning your speaking engagement pricing. It helps you avoid confusion and helps you make sense of the expenses that traveling can incur.

- **Please be flexible.** Humility is both firm and flexible. There are also denominational differences in speaker honorariums. I spoke at a Methodist Church in North Atlanta about the creative arts and scribal ministry not too long ago. Within that particular denominational structure, they had maximum honorariums that speakers received for certain services. They would not budge no matter what! But it is also RARE to be requested into that denomination from a "non-Methodist" background. I had to recognize the prophetic power in that... as well as what the Lord was opening up for me.

Again, it is not always about the money when you are pursuing PURE ministry. They always know what something is worth or might cost for them. Again, I have learned that the apostolic-prophetic community is quite unique and random in its approach. What we consider excellence has a completely different set of rules in other denominations – rules many I know would not be able to receive. Again, investigate before sending expectations and contracts over; and definitely avoid making demands unless you are positioned like Oprah Winfrey, Joel Osteen, Tyler Perry, or T.D. Jakes.

A guest poet or spoken word artist (or any artist that has a 10 to 15-minute role or less) should not expect to receive the same

How to price your scribal ministry

honorarium or financial gift as a keynote speaker in most circumstances. Think of it this way, the people attending the conference or event came to hear the speaker deliver a 45-minute speech or conduct a two to three-hour workshop. The poet provides the inspiration instead. While both are valuable and graceful contributors, the release is not the same. There should never be an expectation for comparable honorariums in this regard. However, if you are the main "event" for a lack of a better description, then your honorarium can be comparable to that of the keynote or workshop presenter depending on your role.

- **Do not demand a certain honorarium amount.** It is important to be clear and firm in your expectations, but never obstinate, arrogant, and demanding. The PROPHETIC carries *tremendous* grace and firmness. For serious inquiries, I send my speaker fee schedule with a note saying, "Fees are negotiable and/or we are willing to work within your conference budget." In my situation, I have a family. A $300 honorarium for an out of town or out of state conference would not cover transportation or gas at the very least.

Let us be real: It would cost me to travel to them and serve. This is not a problem in a mutually edifying relationship, missional service, or volunteering because we are volunteering, serving at our own will with no demands. But in other circumstances, this is not fair to the speaker.

Speaker pricing in ministry environments work differently from speaking in secular environments. Secular simply refers to environments that lack a spiritual focus and can range from academic seminars to non-profit fundraisers. These environments often offer predictable honorarium schedules for speakers, clearer speaker expectations and outlines for what they will and will not provide. However, this is not a throw off on the congregation at all.

It is just that those environments operate on a cut-and-dry process that can be simpler to navigate even though they may be more difficult to break into. It is so important not to bring ministry expectations into secular environments. *They are strikingly different.*

- **Get rid of the selling yourself short mentality.** So many "beginners" suffer from this. It is price gouging in the spirit! Come on, laugh with me. What you bring to the table may be worth $50k but the world cannot see it in you, and some of those people in your current circle of influence may not be able to afford that honorarium. Sometimes the best choice is to enter and serve! Do not be so quick to decline an invitation because it does not fit your vision "for what you are worth" and you feel as if you are selling yourself short.

I run into so many Sons who refuse to consider any engagement that doesn't meet their financial requirements! The key here, however, is making suggestions to come at a later time to give the host an opportunity to build the budget. It's also an opportunity to look at others you may benefit from, that is pleasing to the Lord.

Listen, I had an opportunity to speak at a conference 10 years ago and teach three days on the ministry of the scribe at my own expense (rental car, supplies, gas, babysitter, etc.). They provided housing and meals, and a promised honorarium. I believed in the VISION of that event. I could see what the Lord would do in years to come. So, I made the sacrifice. The connections I made through that opportunity led to the sellout of all of my inventory in one-day, international ministry opportunities, lifelong friendships, and doors that are still opening a decade later. I was not selling myself short but recognizing an opportunity greater than money.

- **You do not need a crowd.** You need the right HEART and the grace to meet the right person or people! I can trace my ministry success in the speaking arena to TWO PEOPLE who opened the door of their ministry and hearts to me. Seriously. About six years ago, I taught at a conference where only three people registered for my scribal workshop. I was ready to cancel in disappointment when I received a call from the conference facilitator saying: "None of your students want to cancel. Can you please come, and still hold the session?" So I did. I gave them my best as if I were teaching before thousands. That session was filled with miracles, signs, wonders, healing, breakthrough, and wide-effective doors. No honorarium could have provided that kind of favor.

Again, speaker pricing in ministry environments are structured differently from those in secular environments. Secular simply refers to organizations or groups whose focus is not on ministry. Think of a community recreation center, a public school, hospital, or university. These environments often offer predictable requirements for speakers as well as honorarium schedules. This is not a throw off on the congregation at all, it is just that those environments operate on a cut-and-dry process for speaking engagements.

It is so important not to bring ministry expectations into secular environments or vice versa. The two are not the same. Be reminded that the way "prophetic communities" schedule speaking engagements is often different from what we would see in denominational groups - Episcopalian to United Methodist. I know, I have spoken in many environments over the years on varying subjects. Many denominations only work with those within their denomination also. How we present ourselves in these different groups can determine the opportunities we would get. Consider having speaker pricing for secular and ministry environments.

Are you willing to develop different speaking styles for different groups? If not, I strongly suggest that you do. We should try to be versatile people. This is difficult for some prophetic people, easy for others. Religious prophetic people often block themselves into one category. They might say, "I only speak at churches or I only speak to youth groups." My advice: Don't be that person.

God really is bigger than that kind of thinking.

Give the Holy Spirit a chance to stretch you. Have some fun and challenge yourself. By being flexible, you can expand your speaking engagements by reaching broader audiences - WITHOUT compromising who you are. One way to break into this is to consider being a part of interdenominational networks, associations, and groups; or join associations, attend small business meetings, writing and arts events, participate in network opportunities etc. The Lord works in our whole lives, not just the ministry parts of it.

SAMPLE SPEAKING TOPICS

Below is a brief list of my speaking topics. Note how I chose three categories: Ministry Maturity & Integrity, God's Purpose for the Worship Arts, and Sexual & Relational Brokenness. Also note that under each category, I included a description of "qualifications" to speak on those topics.

While you do not have to do this, I strongly suggest it. In doing so, you can see not only what you carry, but your investment in what you have and gain some ideas concerning how you can grow and develop. This particular list is for my personal use, not the public. I edited it for use in this book, but my list is way more detailed than this.

Every few months, I review it to see how I have grown and developed. What I did not include but should have are my other credentials which include advanced professional degrees, ministerial licensing, associations, certifications, and memberships. All of these things can add value to how you price speaking engagements. How? Well, they could set you apart from other people. Also, they can prove that your expert knowledge is not assumed, but qualified not only through ministerial experience and calling, but through practical experience and professional training.

Here is my list of speaking topics:

- MINISTRY MATURITY & INTEGRITY
    - Over the past decade, Theresa Harvard Johnson has taught extensively on ministry integrity as it relates to Ephesians 4 ministry gifts. Available collateral includes over 30 teachings on audio and video available for viewing and download, and extensive writings on her personal blog.
        - Immersion & the Spirit of this Age
        - The Responsibility of Sonship
        - The Rewards of Understanding
        - Holiness & Sanctification
        - Ministry Protocol
            - Prophetic Protocol in Leading Others
            - Apostolic Mentorship

- Toxic mentorship & Spiritual Abuse
- Ministry Accountability
- Freedom from Religion & People
- Breaking free of the goat generation

- GOD'S PURPOSE FOR THE WORSHIP ARTS
    - Over the past 15 years, Theresa Harvard Johnson has written over 25 books on scribal ministry, worship, and arts, and taught at hundreds of church conferences and venues in person, online and in her own school of ministry. Collateral includes fully developed online courses, books on the worship arts and scribal ministry, testimonials from global pioneers, television, and radio interviews, etc.
        - Healing Through the Arts
        - Building Scribal Communities
        - Developing a Healthy Scribal Nation®
        - Arts & Community: The Scribal Arts
        - The Role of the Worship Arts in the Church
        - The 21st century release of The Scribal Anointing®

- The Scribal Realm of Dreams & Visions
- The Bezalel Anointing from a Scribal Perspective
- Literary Evangelism, beyond the open mic
- The Academic, Historical & Biblical Realm of the Scribe

- SEXUAL ASSAULT, SEXUAL ABUSE & RELATIONAL BROKENNESS
  - Over the past 20 years, Theresa Harvard Johnson has worked with both Christian and secular organizations to help people heal from sexual trauma through teaching, training, and the expressive arts. As a ward of the state and an overcomer of severe childhood abuse, she has received extensive training in healing through local, national, and international programs for foster children and those sexually exploited. She has 15 years of experience volunteering, serving, partnering, and hosting programs for the broken. Most recently, she released an expressive art project entitled: Humiliation: A Story of Rape through Art & Poetry.

Just because the world has been impacted by the COVID-19

Pandemic, doesn't mean public speaking is a free-for-all. Although those in the event and business industry are at the beginning of their own reformation and reconstruction period, there will always be a need for presenters and facilitators. The difference is that their presence will be virtual. But because we are prophetic scribes, let us think FORWARD not backwards.

There are three things every speaker should do at this point: (1) Learn how to present conferences and workshops professionally online using top-of-the-line-apps; (2) Create home studios, set up rooms in their home for seminars or develop multi-professional backgrounds to use to stream live or pre-record; and (3) Create a seminar atmosphere in their home as opposed to the "sit-down" teaching model. Make the "sit-down" teaching model for speakers' center on discussions and workshops and keep the platform (podium and mic) presentation model for professional speaking.

This may include investing in necessary equipment to create a personal studio of sorts for the best quality video and presentation. Use whiteboards and dry erasers, flip charts, and all the other tools you would use in a regular workshop or seminar setting. Switch things up by getting the latest presentation tools, instead of always using PowerPoint presentations. Still prepare files for download, promotional products that can be mailed out and, maybe go back to writing thank you notes by hand. We may live in a virtual world, but one day we will still need clips of our speaking engagements to share with others that have some versatility.

For those in the public speaking arena, things have and are continuing to shift and change. What they are not doing, however, is dying. The concept is simple: *"Prepare virtually as if you are preparing in person."* If you are hosting an event, find the software and platform that allows the best affordable experience. While we may not be able to gather in large crowds, we can still book a small conference room for major virtual events to set up filming.

SETTING PRICING FOR ONLINE SPEAKING

Virtual events do not change the value of what you bring to the table! If you have children at home and work, it can still affect your personal expenses as well. For example, a babysitter might still be needed, or you may need to take half-a-day off at work to make room for the occasion.

If ever there was a reason to stick with "keeping your set pricing" it is BECAUSE your speaking engagement is virtual and can EASILY, RAPIDLY be repurposed for various uses. We are living in a time when what is "recorded or filmed" could be recycled multiple times by individuals, organizations, and groups for profit long after the assignment is over. In my personal experience, people have repeatedly:

- Packaged and resold my teachings on the scribe

through their ministries and websites

- Placed teachings in paid conferences, events including online schools without permission
- Released private, income generating, proprietary/copyrighted teachings/lectures to the general public
- Marketed CDs & DVDs for sale at other conferences and events without my permission
- Combined lectures with other live events, groups, activities without consent, permission

As far as I am concerned, these are unethical practices and stand outside of FAIR USE within the copyright laws in the United States.

Just because an organization brought a person in to speak, does not necessarily mean that the host OWNS the rights to the speaker's message or materials. There are only two ways in which this would be okay: (1) The speaker grants the individual, organization or group written permission to sell, distribute or market the speaker's message by any means they desire; or (2) You have contracted with that individual, organization or group for distribution rights prior to the speaking engagement.

Listen, if a congregation cannot perform a copyrighted song on Sunday morning live or online without adhering to licensing, how much more applies to the copyrighted content from a lecture or presentation?

In addition, no one knows how to package or represent you or your brand BETTER THAN YOU! No one should have the freedom to randomly sell your products or services without your knowledge or consent.

Again, things like this are understood in the "secular" arena. In the church arena, some denominations adhere to proper protocols and procedures when it comes to these matters - which are legal in nature. However, many people in the apostolic-prophetic community completely disregard them... and will fight you about your own material. I want to remind you that there are many things within our charismatic faith that are unconventional and suspect. The "entitlement" mindset trickles down to people who believe they have overcome it.

SOLUTION: In this season of virtual speaking engagements, add an inquiry on your personal speaker request form that requires potential hosts to choose, "Virtual Event or In-Person." Also add a section that asks, "Do you plan to distribute or promote this lecture after the event? If so, please provide details on how you would like to distribute and promote this lecture after the event." Doing so provides an opportunity to submit a revised agreement to your host and state your expectations clearly. I also place copyright notices and state disclaimers on videos or presentations that I provide stating my expectations and allowances.

DOWNLOAD WORKSHEETS

- Brainstorming Speaking Topics: https://rb.gy/qy1iu8
- Speaking Engagement Categories & Expenses Worksheet: https://rb.gy/jxpmw9

Type the URL into your browser exactly as it appears on this page. Then view or download your file via Google Drive.

MEET THE AUTHOR

Theresa Harvard Johnson is an author and international speaker who is widely known for her revelatory insight, understanding and apostolic teachings on "The Scribal Anointing, the 21st-century revelation of the office of the prophetic scribe.

She has published, contributed to or co-authored more than 22 books including her signature publications, *The Scribal Anointing: Scribes Instructed in the Kingdom of Heaven, The Scribal Realm of Dreams & Visions, and Apostolic Mentorship: Critical Tools to Help Artisans Identify Their God Ordained Mentor.*

Theresa is a former print journalist and a rising historian in the scribal realm. She is burdened to identify, mature, and raise up the Lord's scribal nation while building a repository of revelatory, academic, and historical educational materials that edify and strengthen present day prophetic scribes in their identity, purpose and calling.

In addition, Theresa is committed to maturing the Body of Christ and ensuring that in her realm of influence, Christ is always elevated above people. She holds a MDIV in Biblical Studies and a MAPW from Liberty University. She is also the founder of The Scribal Conservatory Arts & Worship Center and The School of the Scribe based in Atlanta, Georgia (USA).

MORE INFORMATION

The School of the Scribe
950 Eagles Landing Parkway, #302
Stockbridge, GA 30281
Email: theresahj@schoolofthescribe.com
Online School: members.schoolofthescribe.net
Official Website: thescribalanointing.com

RECOMMENDED BOOKS:

- *The Scribal Anointing: Scribes Instructed in the Kingdom of Heaven*
- *The Scribal Companion Student Workbook*
- *Scribal Purpose: 10 Reasons Why God Commanded You to Write*
- *Spiritually Critiquing Literary Works*
- *Literary Evangelism: Beyond the Open Mic*
- *The Sin of Spiritual Plagiarism: Unauthorized Vessels*
- *40 Signs of a Prophetic Scribe*
- *Signs of a Scribal Prophet*
- *The Scribal Realm of Dreams & Visions*
- *The Scribal Realm of Dreams & Visions Dream Journal*
- *Graphic Design & The Prophetic*
- *Writing & the Prophetic*
- *50 Prophetic Writing Prompts to Jumpstart Your Prophetic Writing Flow*
- *50 Indisputable Biblical Facts About the Ministry of the Prophetic Scribe*
- *How to Write an Author Bio*
- *How to Price Your Scribal Ministry Engagements*
- *Apostolic Mentorship: Critical Tools to Help You Identify Your God Ordained Mentor*

- *Humiliation: A story of rape through Art & Poetry*
- *The Scribal Toolkit for Prophetic Scribes*
- *The Beginners Guide to Conducting Professional Interviews*
- *Protecting Your Scribal Projects: Securing Files in a Digital World*
- *The Prophetic Scribe's Blueprint*
- *Starting from Where You Are (Prophetic Documenting)*

www.ingramcontent.com/pod-product-compliance
Lightning Source LLC
Chambersburg PA
CBHW030454220526
45464CB00006B/2528